W9-BLG-726

DISCARD

DATE DUE

DISCARD

MEDIEVAL LIVES

Merchant

ROBERT HULL

A⁺
Smart Apple Media

Smart Apple Media is published by Black Rabbit Books
P.O. Box 3263, Mankato, Minnesota 56002

Printed in the United States

Published by arrangement with the Watts Publishing Group Ltd, London.

Library of Congress Cataloging-in-Publication Data

Hull, Robert, 1935–
    Merchant / Robert Hull.
        p. cm.—(Smart Apple Media. Medieval lives)
    Summary: "Traces the life of a typical merchant in medieval times from birth to death, including childhood, marriage, becoming a successful merchant, and customs. Includes primary source quotes"—Provided by publisher.
        Includes index.
        ISBN 978-1-59920-170-2
        1. Merchants—Europe—History—To 1500—Juvenile literature. I. Title.
    HF395.H85 2009
    381.094'0902—dc22

                                                                    2007046031

Artwork: Gillian Clements
Editor: Sarah Ridley
Editor-in-chief: John Miles
Designer: Simon Borrough
Art director: Jonathan Hair
Picture research: Diana Morris

Picture credits:
Bibliothèque Mazarine, Paris/Archives Charmet/Bridgeman Art Library: 16. Bibliothèque Municipale, Valenciennes / Alfredo Dagli Orti /The Art Archive: 10. Bibliothèque Nationale, Paris/Flammarion/Bridgeman Art Library: 11. Bibliothèque Universitaire de Mèdecine, Montpellier/Gianni Dagli Orti/The Art Archive: 40. British Library, London/The Art Archive: front cover, 23, 32, 37. British Library Board, London, All Rights Reserved/Bridgeman Art Library: 29. British Library, London/HIP/Topfoto: 9b, 14, 17, 21, 27, 30, 36, 39tl, 39tr. Castello di Issogne Valle d'Aosta/Giraudon/Bridgeman Art Library: 38. Collegio del Cambio, Perugia/Gianni Dagli Orti/The Art Archive: 5, 9t. Koninklijk Museum voor Schone Kunsten, Antwerp/Bridgeman Art Library: 20. Museo de Arte Antiga, Lisbon/Gianni Dagli Orti/the Art Archive: 33. Musée Condé, Chantilly/Giraudon/Bridgeman Art Library: 41. Museo Correr, Venice/Alfredo Dagli Orti/The Art Archive: 28. Osterreichische Nationalbibliothek, Vienna/Alinari/Bridgeman Art Library: 24. 35.m Palazzo Medici-Riccardi, Florence/Bridgeman Art Library: 8bl, 19. Palazzo Pubblico, Siena/ Alfredo Dagli Orti/The Art Archive: 13. Private Collection/Bridgeman Art Library: 25. Charles Walker/Topfoto: 15t.

9 8 7 6 5 4 3 2 1

CONTENTS

INTRODUCTION

The medieval period of European history is from approximately 1000 to 1500. It was a time of momentous events. In 1066, England was conquered by the Norman French duke, William, and his men. William was crowned king in December 1066. During most of the fourteenth century, France and England fought a series of wars called the Hundred Years' War. In addition, Christian crusaders fought Muslim Arab armies over the control of Jerusalem. The Black Death, or plague, in 1348, killed about one-third of the population of Europe, altering the balance of society.

Feudal Society

At the beginning of this period, European society was feudal. Kings owned all the land, but a class of knights was granted land in return for service in war. Knights made similar arrangements with holders of manorial estates and they, in turn, with those below them. This continued down to the peasants, who were granted a few acres of land to farm, to which they were tied, in return for fees and heavy service obligations. This network of agreements held society together.

A network of services and obligations held feudal society together. Merchants, however, were outside of this structure.

Safe, walled towns such as this were good for trade.

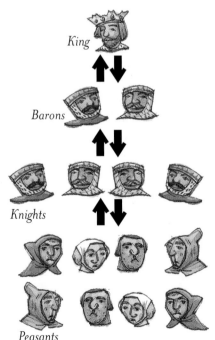

King

Barons

Knights

Peasants

A merchant writes a letter, while an assistant stands by.

Throughout the medieval period, great projects such as monasteries and abbeys, houses, colleges, castles, churches, and cathedrals were built.

Towns and Trade

From the thirteenth century onward, there was a rapid development of trade. Society became less feudal, as rents paid in money took the place of many services. Money payments also took over from exchange or payments in kind. The ability to buy items with money spread to all groups except the poorest. Gradually, many peasants became more free from feudal services and fees. They bought land, became artisans—skilled workers—and moved to towns.

Towns grew in number and size, led by a prosperous class of burgesses—merchants who made their living in national and international trade. Certain features that became modern banking techniques began to develop, particularly in Italy. Banks agreed to treat a piece of paper with a promise to pay as the equivalent of silver or gold. This was the forerunner of the check.

Farming

But the medieval world was still an agricultural world. Most people worked on the land to feed themselves. They would take any surplus produce to market. They used the money they earned to buy household items such as garden tools, pottery, or clothes that they did not make themselves. They might buy these from traveling merchants or "chapmen."

The Wool Merchant

The export of wool from England, Spain, and northern Africa to the weaving looms of Italy and Flanders was one of the great trading phenomena of medieval times. Merchants in England made fortunes by buying wool produced in wool-growing districts and selling it to cloth merchants from Europe.

This is the story of a typical medieval person who was born into a family of shopkeepers but who became a prosperous merchant.

A wealthy merchant on his horse.

FIRST DAYS

The woman has worked downstairs in the family shop during her pregnancy. She has come up to the bedroom to give birth, helped by a midwife and women neighbors. The women wash the newborn boy carefully with warm water and rub him down gently with a mixture of roses and salt. A finger dipped in honey is rubbed in his mouth. They wrap him in swaddling clothes, long strips of cloth. They believe this will help his limbs grow straight.

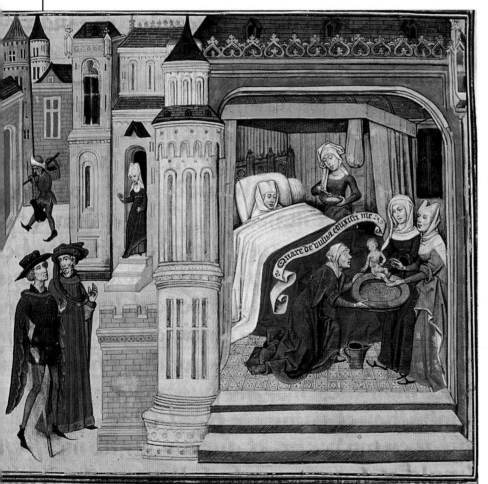

As richly dressed visitors approach the house, female servants and relatives see to washing the new baby.

Baptism

Baptism into the church comes next in his life. This baby is healthy, but if he had not been, the midwife would have performed the actions of baptizing him as she has been taught to do. It would be done quickly because the priest and the church teach that a child who dies unbaptized will not go to heaven.

Being healthy though, he is taken to the church with as many family and friends as can be there—but perhaps not his mother. He is baptized at the big stone font. The priest speaks the words that bring the baby into the lifelong care of the church and sprinkles holy water on him. One of the three godparents names him.

Medieval Facts

The figures relating to the mortality of medieval royal babies, children, and young people make sad reading. Royal babies and children had the best care available then, but of the approximately 96 children born to the kings and queens of England between 1150 and 1500, about 34 died in their first year. An additional 22 died before they were 20. The figure of 96 does not include stillborn babies or those who died at birth. Plague and war caused a few of the deaths.

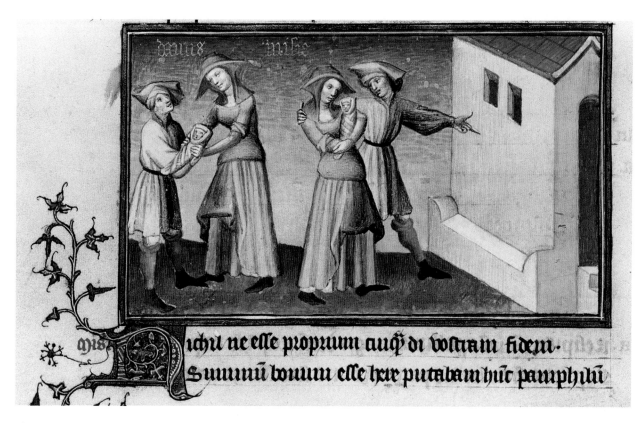

The husband accompanies his wife to the churching ceremony.

When the mother is strong enough to go out, she is churched at a service of purification. The church believes that giving birth, being fleshly and unspiritual, is a contaminating process.

Sleep and Nourishment

The baby's food is his mother's milk until he's nearly three. He doesn't drink cow's milk or water because they are not really safe. His solid food is chewed for him, or strained, in his mother's mouth first.

The baby sleeps in a cradle. When he is older, his mother will let him share a bed with his brothers and sister. When he is weaned (no longer breast-fed), he will sit at the table to eat. His father and mother use wooden armchairs; the children sit on stools. They all wear hats, to help keep warm, even at the table.

The older children are gently hit when they behave badly at the table. Their parents repeat what the books about children's table manners say: don't wipe your nose on the tablecloth, don't wriggle, and don't gulp your food.

Medieval Facts

In some parts of Europe, it was believed that fireflies were the souls of unbaptized babies.

Medieval Facts

The mothers of babies who became sick often tried religious or superstitious remedies. One method was to carefully measure the sick child's height and present a candle of the same height as an offering at a shrine. Sick children also might be taken to a saint's tomb and laid there for a while. In one case, a baker from Canterbury borrowed a garment that was said to have saint's blood on it. He washed it in water and gave the water to his son to drink. The boy recovered.

HOUSE AND HOME

The downstairs part of the young boy's house is a shop, where his father and mother sell hats, caps, and other items such as thread and ribbon, beads and cheap ornaments, and even paper and some board games. The shop is open fronted, but at night his parents close a shutter over the counter.

Medieval Facts

There is evidence from wills about the household objects that artisan shopkeepers owned. One fifteenth-century barber's will lists: 12 silver spoons, a featherbed and bedclothes, 6 pewter plates, a brass pot, fire irons, a chest of spruce wood, 4 candlesticks, rosary beads, and a saddle and bridle. The mention of these items in a will means they were valuable to the owner. He will have possessed other items which he valued, but not enough to mention them in a will, such as furniture, tablecloths, and clothes.

A group of shops with outside counters and living quarters over the shop.

following guild rules, an apprentice sleeps at night. Steep stairs lead up to a small first-floor living area and bedroom.

During the day, the young child wanders around the shop and back room, watched by his mother. He plays while she shows goods to possible customers, sews things for sale, or sees to the cooking or other household tasks.

Living in a Shop

Behind the shop area, another room reaches up two stories to roof height. The fire warms the house and is used for cooking. The smoke rises and goes out under the tiles or through the window openings.

The room is also a storage place and a workshop for making things they sell. There are benches and stools, a trestle table for display, a board with counters for making calculations, and ladders to reach the shelves and cupboards. In the corner is a small bed where,

Town Houses

This house is one of the first in the town to be built in a row of three, with another shop next door. This new arrangement makes building cheaper, but if a fire breaks out in one wooden house, it will spread to the others quickly. Fires can devastate whole areas of towns, even destroy them. The town's new regulations ensure this house has a roof of slates, not thatch.

In front of the shop is a noisy, dirty street. It is, though, less cluttered than it used to be and cleaner. There are new regulations against leaving piles of timber or heaps of manure in the street or digging holes in the street. This helps the shop's trade.

Dirt and Refuse

The town has men to carry refuse away. They empty the backyard midden or refuse heap and the cesspit that collects waste from the indoor privy or lavatory. The street is still smelly, but it used to be worse. Not even the worst smells wake up sleeping toddlers. Noise, though, does, and the street is very noisy. Horses and carts pass through all day long; traders call out nonstop. There's a continuous din from the cooked-foods shop next door, the forge, the carpenters' shops further on, and from the tavern and market stalls. When that quiets down, there are still the church bells. The toddler can pop his head out the front of the shop for a while, as long as

someone is keeping an eye on him. His mother takes him to the market stalls with her, too. He starts to see the town.

A street in Siena, as painted in about 1340, showing packhorses, sheep, and merchants trading, with glimpses of indoor scenes, including a teacher at a desk.

fter the shop is closed, there is still work to do. But there is also entertainment by the fireside such as telling stories or playing board games.

A man and a woman pass the time with a board game.

Wandering the Town

There are no parks, but the young boy has the town to wander in. He can throw sticks in the stream, build little dams, or catch stickleback fish. He can play with a ball in the street, walk along walls, or climb piles of wood.

He is free to roam these streets near home, but animals use them too. There is always danger from horses' hooves, cows' horns, and pigs with sharp teeth who have escaped their pens and are running about. There are risks from being too adventurous as well. Youngsters have drowned in millponds or by falling off bridges and into the river.

Games

There are games to play with friends, brothers, and sisters: hide-and-seek, tag, and hobbyhorse. As he grows older, he joins the grown-ups in various boisterous sports: football, cockfighting, wrestling, archery, and even pretend battles with spears. In winter, young and old skate and play games together on the ice.

There is other entertainment that also appeals to the growing boy, such as mystery plays. These are performed by members of craftmen's guilds and retell stories from the Bible.

Fairs

There is a market in the town and sometimes a fair with traveling entertainers such as *gestours*, who perform story-poems with great bravura and gesturing, and jugglers and minstrels, and *podicicinists*, or wind-breakers—an entertainment his parents frown on.

A group playing cards.

History shows some things don't change. Bartholomeus Anglicus, a thirteenth-century French writer, described children's behavior:

❖ *They want everything they see and beg for it with voice and hand... When they be washed they are so dirty again. When their mother washes and combs them, they kick and sprawl, and put out their hands, and resist with all their might. They are always wanting a drink; they are no sooner out of bed than they are crying for something to eat.* ❖

Another entertainment parents frown on is the habit boys have on winter festival days of going through the town dressed up, singing songs, and asking for money or food. It's fun for boys though.

Some other kinds of fun are seasonal, such as autumnal scrumping (stealing fruit off trees), playing soccer with the bladders of newly slaughtered pigs in November, and, of course, snowball fights in winter.

SCHOOL

The boy's parents know if he is to succeed in trade, their son must learn to read and write. When they signed the agreement for their oldest son to become an apprentice, the master craftsman promised to teach him reading, writing, and grammar. Their daughter is beginning to learn her alphabet too, taught at home by her mother. Their younger son needs to go to school.

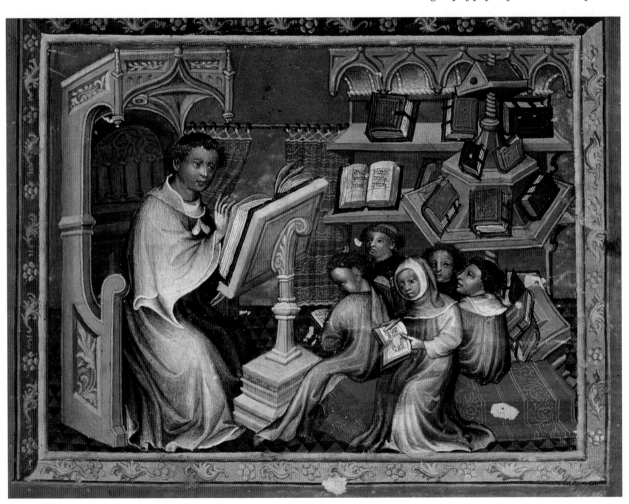

Going to School

The town's schoolmaster teaches the boys in his house. Early every morning, the shopkeeper's son puts on his stockings, shoes, tunic, and belt. He collects his penner that holds his writing quills, his knife, and his horn tube containing ink. He carries these in his belt and brings his own candle because it will be dark in the schoolroom. He quickly runs off through the cold streets to be there by seven A.M. and pay the fee. He will be at school all day, until late afternoon, though he will have two hour-or-more breaks, one at about ten A.M. and another at lunchtime.

The boys learn the alphabet and begin to memorize, then read aloud The Lord's Prayer, The Ten Commandments, and other religious pieces. They read from a much-used, worn primer, which is a book written out by hand by the schoolmaster or perhaps by a monk from the nearby monastery.

Reading

The boy reads at first by rote—from memory—without understanding. It is boring, but he tries hard because if he makes mistakes he is likely to be beaten. He is lucky that he is learning his own language first, rather than Latin, as children once did. Later, he will learn to read some Latin too, including verse by memory and a book of grammar.

He learns to write by scratching his letters on a waxed tablet. Occasionally, he uses ink on scraps of parchment. He learns to count, using counters placed on a cloth with lines marking columns for units, tens, hundreds, and so on. He has to calculate answers to simple questions of arithmetic.

A teacher of geometry with instruments and shapes.

BECOMING A MERCHANT

Now that he is 16, the young man wants to become prosperous. He believes the way to do this is to buy and sell what people cannot do without. He sees that the goods that produce wealth for individuals in his town are either luxuries that well-off people need—French and Spanish wines, spices, or expensive cloths and fabrics—or ordinary goods that are always needed, because they are consumed or wear out, such as clothes and shoes. He would like to be a merchant eventually, but he decides that the way to start is with cheap, necessary goods, not luxuries.

Traveling merchants, or chapmen, went between towns on horseback.

whatever he can buy inexpensively in the town and sell in the village for a small profit.

He does well and buys a packhorse. He is robbed once, in the forest, and loses woolen cloths of various colors and a pack of shoes. He has to buy another supply of cloth and clothing goods and start on his travels again. He loads his horse up with shoes, purses, hats, chemises (shirts), some three-penny tunics for landless serfs, cloth for peasant tunics, fine

The Chapman's Life

The young man decides to try life as a chapman, or peddler, traveling the winding tracks between farms, villages, and towns, selling at houses, markets, and fairs. Off he goes on foot, the sack on his back stuffed with anything from ribbons, knives, and decorated belts to shoes and herbal remedies:

It became common practice to share the cost and risks of exporting goods by sea. The following quote is from a partnership document written in 1248 that records an agreement to share the cost and risk of hiring, buying, or constructing ships to carry goods between Marseilles and Genoa:

❖ *I, James Lavagne, acknowledge to you, William Cadenet, citizen of Marseilles, that I have bought for you under your name, at Genoa, a sixth part in a certain ship which is called St. Leonard, at a price of forty-one (Genoese) pounds and two solidi and six denarii in which Hugh Quillian and William Sansier are partners with me. And I bought a thirty-third part in a ship called the St. Agnes, at a price of fifty (Genoese) pounds, in which ship Bonvassal Castel and his associates are partners.* ❖

wool cloth, and a little silk cloth. He uses all the daylight he can, in summer and winter. He does not dawdle in taverns. He has a cheery smile for the peasant women in their gardens and a tickle under the chin for their toddlers. Villagers welcome him. After a year's successful traveling, he is confident about the future.

Expanding Horizons

The young man buys another horse and adds pans, pottery, and gardening tools to his wares. Occasionally, he even hires a boat to carry heavy goods such as iron farming implements up rivers to sell in towns and along the coast. He meets other traders at markets and fairs and gets to know some merchants.

He has saved almost enough money to set himself up as a merchant when he takes a great risk. He puts most of his savings in a ninth share of a ship traveling with wool, grain, and fish to the great port of Bruges.

His risk pays off. No pirates raid the ship, no storms assail it, and the vessel arrives safely in port.

The Journey of the Magi, *as painted by Benozzo Gozzoli in the 1460s, is seen as a journey of traders over a mountain pass with packhorses and camels.*

MARRIAGE

T he young man was still only a boy of 14 when his parents received a suggestion from the godmother of a young girl of 11. Would they consider their son's engagement to her goddaughter? The girl was from a respectable draper's family who wished her to be settled in marriage in a few years time.

The boy's parents thought that it was too soon to be thinking about such things; the lad was still no more than a dreamy boy.

Dowry Worries

Marriage arrangements relating to gifts and dowries had to satisfy both sets of parents. Margery Brews writes anxiously to John Paston III (1477) that her father will not give more than he has already promised:
❖ *My mother has worked hard with my father but she cannot get any more money than you know about, and, God knows, I am very sorry about it. But if you love me, as I hope you do, you will not leave me. For if you had only half the wealth you have, I would not leave you.* ❖

A wedding ceremony outside the church door with the priest officiating.

Betrothal

Four years later, the matter is raised again. This time, it seems a good business arrangement for both families. The amount that the girl's father says he is willing to give her as a dowry to take into the marriage seems satisfactory. Now it will be wise to see if the 18-year-old boy and the 15-year-old girl are happy in each other's company.

The couple spend some time together, and when it seems that they are well suited, relatives and friends are gathered to hear the girl's father promise the young merchant-to-be her hand in marriage. The families' representatives shake hands on the contract, which includes details of the dowry she will bring to the marriage. The couple plight their troth with a handfasting.

A few weeks later, after the priest has announced the banns three times in church, the wedding ceremony takes place at the church door. The bride is formally presented to her future father-in-law; the groom places the ring on the bride's finger. They enter the church for a nuptial (wedding) mass. That same evening, the wedding banquet is held at the bride's parents' house.

Wedding

Special cooks have been hired and servants wear uniforms. Large amounts of food are served, but the bride hardly eats. At the end, gifts are presented and music plays. A child is placed in the bride's lap, and a gold coin is placed in her shoe. The child symbolizes fertility; the coin symbolizes riches.

Afterward, a noisy procession follows the couple back to the house. There is singing, giggling, and a joke in poor taste: the bride is told that her husband of an hour has ridden away on his horse—scared at the whole idea of marriage to her!

A medieval party—wedding guests dance to bagpipes and tabor, a small drum.

THE WOOL TRADE

The successful married chapman has become a wool merchant, making expensive, lengthy, and sometimes hazardous journeys to buy newly sheared wool, transport it to a market, and sell it. He rides to the Cotswolds, Oxfordshire, where he believes the best wool is to be found. English wool, the most expensive, is the wool that Flemish and Italian cloth makers want to make into the best quality cloth. Cheaper wool can be purchased from the Italian hills, if he wished to travel there, or Spain and North Africa.

The merchant shares a meal with his suppliers.

Buying in the Cotswolds

In the towns of Burford and Northleach, he meets men who have tended sheep all their working lives. He has a business arrangement with two sheep farmers from whom he buys the summer's clip of wool and the autumn's harvest time crop of fells, the wool and skins of sheep slaughtered and salted down for winter meat.

Over a drink, this year's deal is made. The wool will be checked for quality, ensuring that nothing worthless is mixed with it—no hair or straw. Each huge sack is labeled, numbered, and sealed. It is then loaded on wagons or in sarplers (half-sacks) on the backs of packhorses for the slow journey to London or to one of the small ports on the south coast. At the ports, the collectors of customs for the king record the names of merchants shipping wool, the amounts, and the quality.

The different activities of sheep farming; shearing is depicted in the foreground.

Crossing the English Channel

The ship that sails for Calais from one of the small south-coast ports is one of the smaller ships, 110 tons (100 tonnes). On board are about 20 sailors, men ready to fight off pirates with bows and arrows, cannon, and gunpowder. The crossing might take three days. It might—if there are storms—take two weeks, or even more.

It is a great relief when journeys are accomplished safely in only a few days—with no pirates, no storms, no fires on board, and nothing lost overboard.

The Staple at Calais

It was not always the case, but all English wool now ships to Calais, except smuggled wool and the

wool bought by Italian merchants who can export directly to Italy by ship. Calais—then owned by England— is where the fourteenth-century staplers had their headquarters. This group of merchants controlled the English wool trade.

In Calais, the wool is checked again, one sample sack is opened and the seal broken. The stapler must check that the wool is what the labels say it is and that none of the sacks have been tampered with or relabeled. Custom, in money, and subsidy, in wool, is then collected for the English monarch.

The wool is ready for sale. Flemish, German, Burgundian, and Italian merchants are waiting. First, they must change their coins into English money. There is a mint at Calais that makes the English gold coins that non-English merchants will have to buy before they purchase wool. Only then can they carry it onward, to the towns of the cloth makers.

The merchant avoids time-consuming journeys if he can. His business is often better served by hard work in the office and counting house. Even so, the wool trade often takes him not only across the Channel to Calais but sometimes further. He travels to markets at Antwerp and Paris, to Avignon, over the Alps to the commercial towns of Italy— Florence, Venice, and Genoa.

TRAVEL AND COMMUNICATION

Weeks and months of the merchant's life are spent traveling. And though the fastest messenger, by changing horses, can make about 100 miles (160 km) in a day, a caravan of horses carrying goods averages no more than 15 miles (25 km) or so. If the merchant travels the length of France, it is a 20-day trip; crossing the Alps takes 5 to 7 days; Paris to Naples, over the Alps, is a 5-week journey.

Tolls and Towns

Slow travel is made slower and trading more expensive by all the local tolls and taxes the merchant has to pay: river tolls, bridge tolls, tolls on setting up stands, and tolls on loading up ships. On great rivers, such as the Seine and the Rhine, there are tolls every 5 to 6 miles (8 to 10 km). Sometimes, the tolls are not legal—a kind of robbery.

The merchant travels from town to town, very slowly by our standards, covering perhaps 25 to 30 miles (40 to 50 km) a day. He passes through villages on the way but prefers to be inside town walls at night. He has to arrive before the gate shuts and the curfew bell tolls. Up the main street he rides, past shops while dodging signs and stakes. He guides his horse around slaughtered animals, piles of

A traveler and his assistant arrive at a tavern, to be greeted by a glass of wine.

Illegal Tolls

An eleventh-century French lord admitted to stopping merchants and exacting tribute, a payment in goods:

❖ *I have stopped the merchants of Langres who passed through my domain. I took merchandise from them and kept it until the Bishop of Langres and the Abbot of Cluny demanded reparation. I had kept part for myself and restored the rest. To get back what I had taken and be able to cross my land in future without fear, they agreed to pay me tribute.* [This did not please the churchmen. Eventually they found a compromise]: *To buy off this exaction and to assure safety to travelers, they have agreed to give me 300 sous.* ❖

A traveler eats a meal at a comfortable tavern while the cook stirs a pot hanging over the fire. (From a late fifteenth-century woodcut.)

The house of rest

manure, and holes in the road. He fends off barking dogs to find his way down narrow passageways toward the market square and the inn.

Inns

In the inns where the merchant stays the night, there are usually several beds in a room. Only occasionally can he have a room to himself. Sometimes he has to share a bed with other travelers. When they arrive, his servant asks about the cleanliness of the rooms, in particular whether there are bugs, fleas, rats, or mice. Of course,

he will be told there aren't any. His horse will be fed and watered in the stables below the inn.

He eats supper with the other guests in the single eating room, among the regulars spending an evening drinking, gambling, singing, and telling tales. Next morning, breakfast is a little bread and beer or water, or cake soaked

in wine. He pays the bill and remembers to ask the innkeeper the way to the next town; there are no signs to help him.

Medieval Facts

This grim little story was related by a thirteenth-century Italian writer. A merchant arrived late at an inn. In the small inn, there were two men to every bed—except for one, with only one occupant who was dead. The merchant, unaware of this, got in beside him, found himself short of room in the bed, and pushed out his bedfellow. The merchant, seeing him lying there dead, believed he had killed him.

Medieval Facts

Walking through medieval towns could be unpleasant. Medieval sanitation was primitive. Big houses might have cesspits for sewage, but in England, only London had a system of conveying waste away: by means of underground wooden pipes. A gutter—or "kennel"—ran down the middle of the streets to carry water away. Travelers had to beware of chamberpots being emptied from upstairs windows, with the cry, "Gardy loo!"—from the French, *Gardez l'eau*: "Look out for the water!"

WAR AND PIRACY

Inns and tolls are irritating nuisances, but not usually hazardous. Apart from the risk of plague, the greatest problems for merchants are the constant wars and the risk of physical attack from pirate ships at sea and bands of brigands, or bandits, on land. Carrying goods on rough routes through forests, over swampy marshland, and across mountains is arduous and risky. Gangs of thieves roam everywhere, especially in times of war.

Pirates

Even in peaceful times, pirates scour the trading routes in the Channel, the North Sea, and the Mediterranean. It is often wiser for ships to travel together in small convoys of six or seven. Otherwise, exports might be banned altogether for the sake of security. The merchant plans his trading journeys carefully.

Pirate Danger

An Italian merchant's letter referred to the perilously pirate-infested stretch of sea between mainland Spain and Majorca:
❖ *The* [pirate] *galley from Peniscola is in these seas, and they say she is bound for Majorca. God sink her speedily. I have goods to send to Barcelona and Majorca and they cannot sail on account of her.* ❖

Under Attack

A merchant ship sailing from Portofino to Pisa, Italy, met two pirate ships at the mouth of the River Arno, but repelled them. The merchant ship went on upriver, trumpets and bagpipes sounding. A short distance from Pisa:
❖ *...by the order of Ser Jacopo, thief and traitor, we came under fire from bowmen hidden in houses and in thickets along the bank, shooting arrows and bombards.* ❖
Local people joined in, and the merchant ship turned back.

War was disastrous for trade. Two opposing armies wait while discussions take place.

Robbers

On land, bad roads and run-down bridges make travelers easy prey for robbers. Bridges regularly fall into disrepair. When those responsible—often the lords of the manor—refuse to act, bridges fall into the river or are closed.

There are no signs. Sometimes, the only way of knowing where the twists and turns of a route are meant to take you is by noting the marks made on trees, branches, and stones.

The Worst Enemy

War is the worst enemy of trade. In these times, war between nations and within them is similiar to a disease that breaks out here or there without warning. When it does, merchants can either call a halt to their business or carry on in the hope that the armies will not cross their route or steal their goods.

In wartime, rulers also need money to pay and equip soldiers, to pay off ransoms, or to pay conquerors. They can raise a tax or obtain a loan. For English kings, a tax on wool is the obvious remedy. Loans from rich Italian wool merchants will help, too. If they are reluctant to lend, their exports can be banned or permission to trade can be withdrawn. In wartime, any merchant established in a foreign city is at risk.

These hazards are real and dramatic. But there is always one other risk on the merchant's mind. Not so dramatic, but just as real, is the chance of being cheated: being sold old wool for new, poor quality for best, or being swindled trying to work out the complicated rates of exchange.

SECRETS OF SUCCESS

The young merchant is prospering. He buys his wool from the Cotswold sheep farmers who are trustworthy and reliable. They produce some of the best wool in England—which also means the best in Europe. Since he buys his wool from them every year, they also trust him.

The cloth merchants who buy wool from him—Italian, Flemish, French, and German—also find him reliable. He means what he says in his letters; he delivers what he promises.

Merchants and traders needed accurate weights to deliver what they promised.

Keeping Up-to-Date

He has kept up-to-date with modern developments in commerce. He worked hard to master the intricate and difficult matter of working out the values of different currencies. He now does it much more quickly because he has learned to calculate using the new numerals from the Muslim world. The ease of using these numbers means he does not have to use counters to work out exchange values or tolls or to write and check bills.

He knows about the new approaches of some Italian bankers. They do more than simply exchange money. They take it and keep it safely on deposit for their clients. They can transfer it to other banks. They are willing to pay money to someone on the strength of seeing his signature on a note, even when he is not present. He has even become a banker himself, in a modest way, lending money to other traders, though not to rulers to help pay for wars. He knows merchants who have been ruined by a king's failure to pay a loan off after losing a war.

Good Sense and Some Luck

Other traits of character have helped him become successful. He has been cautious; he has insured all his cargoes and sent reliable servants with them. He has not expected huge profits on massive deals but a modest level of profit on his routine trading. He pays taxes and subsidies promptly. He also has learned some Italian and

The successful merchant must have been a shrewd judge of people. The Italian merchant Datini lived in permanent fear not only of plague, war, banishment, and political upheaval but also of treacherous dealing. He gives this advice to a colleague:

❖ *You are young, but when you have lived as long as I have and traded with many people, you will know that man is a dangerous creature, and that there is danger in dealing with him.* ❖

can speak with the Italian traders and bankers who live in Southampton and London. His French is good enough to allow him to speak with French merchants, too.

He is prompt and scrupulous in his correspondence and willing to pay a messenger or common carrier. Many rough drafts of letters are written. It all takes time.

He takes no risks traveling and always makes use of a guide in unknown territory, even on short journeys. His success is partly due to skill and hard work. With all this, he has been fortunate so far. His trade has not been seriously impeded by war. He has missed the worst of the floods, and none of his ships has yet sunk.

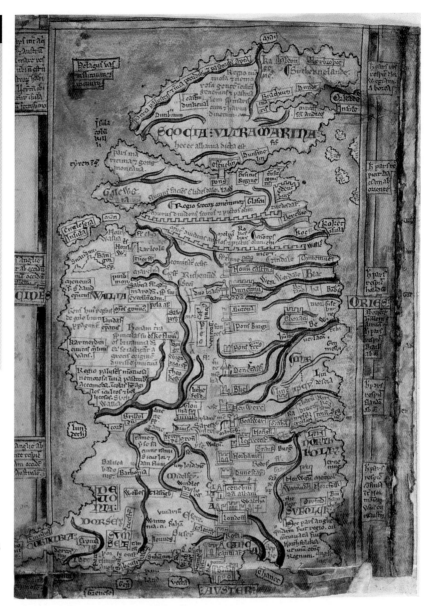

This medieval map of Britain shows how important rivers were to the merchant. The map is vague by our standards, but was very useful.

Medieval merchants had to deal in a bewildering variety of currencies. They needed to know the value of coins such as the French crown, the Milan groat, the English florin and pound, the Burgundy rider, the Scottish guilder, the Florentine florin, the ducat of Venice, and more. There were small coins, like the denarius, or penny. Its value varied depending on how much valuable metal was used.

BRANCHING OUT

The years of traveling abroad to sell wool have taught the merchant many things. One is that making cloth may be more profitable than selling wool. He decides that he will use the wool he buys to make and sell cloth himself. This way, he will avoid the expense, risk, and hard work involved in exporting wool. Wool is not selling as quickly as it once was; there is too much of it for sale, perhaps. In addition, there is a smaller export tax on cloth—3 percent rather than 25 percent.

The Wife of Bath

One of the most memorable characters in Chaucer's *The Canterbury Tales* is the Wife of Bath. She is a successful manufacturer of woven cloth.

❖ *Of clooth-makyng she hadde swich an haunt*
She passed hem of Ypre and of Gaunt. ❖

The fact that her business is superior to those of Flanders, in Ypre (Yrpes) and Gaunt (Ghent), suggests the importance of the English cloth industry.

Two women workers weave cloth.

Stages in Cloth Manufacturing

1. Shearing

4. Weaving

Making Cloth

An important factor affecting his decision is that cloth making now is well-established locally. The rivers and streams provide water for the steps that require it: the cleaning, dyeing, and fulling (beating the cloth). Fulling is now done mechanically in riverside mills.

The other processes are available locally too: carding and combing the tangled dirty wool, spinning it into yarn, weaving the yarn into cloth, and dyeing the cloth. Since each trade has its established guild in the town, the merchant joins the cloth sellers guild.

Whether or not local cloth makers can produce anything to rival beautiful Flemish tapestries is another matter. The main consideration is profit.

Shop

The merchant opens a shop. He sells finished cloth, as well as silks, velvet, and tapestries. He stocks

items related to fabrics and the implements needed to make cloth items: thread, scissors, knives, and hammers. He sells imported plant dyes: madder (red), woad (blue), weld (yellow). He also sells the alum needed for the fabric to hold a dye.

His success gives him confidence. He opens a second shop, which sells goods imported from Spain, Africa, and the Mediterranean: leather from Tunis and Cordoba, sword blades from Toledo, maps from Barcelona, ivory tusks, ostrich feathers, and eggs from the Barbary Coast. His wares now are even more varied than the chapman's wares he once sold.

2. Carding

3. Spinning yarn

5. Dyeing

6. Fulling

WEALTH AND PROPERTY

Wealth and success have come to the merchant. His time is increasingly spent not in planning how to make money but in planning how to spend it. As well as shops, he possesses one or two small houses in addition to his own. He is wealthy enough to buy town properties as they come on the market.

His recently purchased house, set in its own garden and orchard space a short distance from his main shop, is full of expensive wall hangings, pictures, and beautiful furniture, some of which are draped with Italian silks. Some of the most stunning wall coverings, tapestries from Arras, are kept in chests and brought out on feast days and special occasions.

A fifteenth-century view of a prosperous northern European town showing wealthy merchants' houses and a splendid walled garden in the foreground.

Farming

The Italian merchant Datini bought a farm near Prato. In November 1407, he went there:

❖ ...to get the sowing done and the olives picked. But he found that farming at a distance was not easy:
...I stayed there till nightfall without food or drink — I had to shout at the men about a number of things... Meo the foreman is not there, and I think nothing will get done unless I am there myself; the time for sowing is slipping by, and the olives are falling into ditches and getting carried away. ❖

A meal by the fireside in the merchant's warm and welcoming farmhouse in winter.

Furnishings

Most rooms have mirrors. Some vases, jugs, and bowls are made of silver. There is fine furniture throughout the house. Window openings have glass, and one bedroom has stained glass depicting a well-known story. Featherbeds include canopies and footboards. Truckle (trundle) beds are provided for the servants.

The house also has been improved. Now, there is an indoor privy (toilet). Chimneys have been built to channel smoke from the fires out of the house. The main fire in the hall burns coal.

The hall is the merchant family's main living space, but there are stairs to a gallery and upstairs rooms. The hall walls are painted with biblical scenes and episodes from poets' stories.

The merchant has paid for a tiled floor to be laid in the hall, rather than using rushes. One expensive carpet is usually draped over a table. There are also benches, stools, a screen, fire irons, and bellows around the fireplace.

A Farm

The merchant has always liked the idea of having a farm in the country. He has bought pieces of land here and there and is now negotiating to buy the large farmhouse 3 to 4 miles (5 to 6 km) outside the town. Going out there to make plans about orchards and vineyards, herb gardens, and a pasture takes up more and more of his time.

MERCHANT'S WIFE

The merchant's wife no longer helps in the shop. Her work there is done by apprentices and journeymen assistants. She is also aware of her social position: wives of rich merchants do not help in the shop. But now she probably works even harder. She is in charge not only of an expanding household, including servants and children, but also, when her husband is away, of the business itself. She oversees his workers, deals with some of the correspondence, and checks on the running of the shops.

Seated in her comfortable home by a splendid roaring fire and dressed in expensive fabrics, the merchant's wife has good reason to be pleased with her husband's success.

Running the Household

Running the house means buying food and drink and anything else that might be needed, from clothes to garden tools to wall hangings and paintings. It means supervising all the daily household work, from basic cleaning and washing to sewing and embroidery. The merchant's wife does some weaving herself and checks that the brewing and candle making is done properly.

She supervises the servants she has hired, going through the large house checking on their work. She is in and out of the kitchen all day long—the cooks need watching.

Books of Advice

The long day leaves her little time for reading one of the books in which writers advise the wives of merchants how to run a household economically and efficiently. The books suggest that wives should train servants, buy and budget sensibly, and make sure that the house is so pleasant that the husband will always want to bring his friends home. Then, at the end of his life, he will be aware of how much she has done for him. He will be sure to leave his house and household goods to her in his will.

A merchant in fourteenth-century Paris, France, wrote a book for his younger wife, advising and instructing her on how she should be a good wife to him and to the young man she would marry after his death! He wrote that when she goes out to church or into the town, she should be with her *duenna* or maid, and she should behave modestly:

❖ *...walking with head up, eyes lowered and quiet and looking straight in front of you on the ground, looking at neither man nor woman and stopping to speak to no-one in the street.* ❖

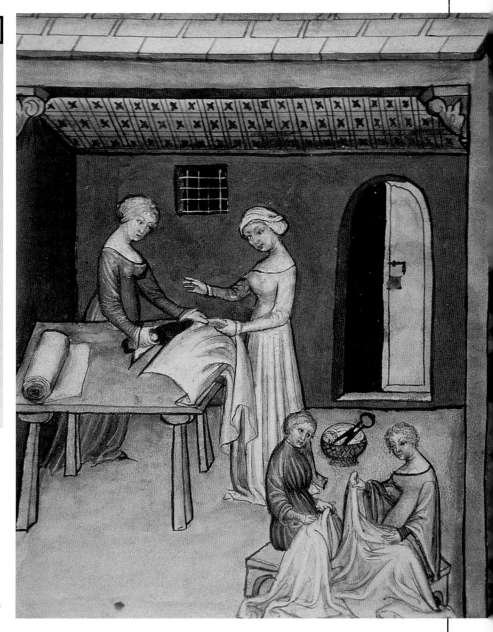

An Italian merchant's wife cuts cloth for a customer.

She hardly needs to be reminded that she should go early to mass, say her prayers quietly, and share meat and wine with the poor—or that she should also know how to get rid of fleas, clean heavy, fur-trimmed garments, keep the weeds from the garden, and make sure there are no holes in the fence for children to creep in and steal the fruit.

And the Children

As if that were not enough, children always need tending. They have been brought up carefully in her care. Servants have helped by looking out for them and accompanying them into town sometimes. But the mother has had the responsibility for seeing to their food and clothing, beginning to teach them how to read and write, and instructing them in religious matters to ensure they learn their prayers and say them.

With her husband, she has arranged for their son's schooling and selected women who come to the house to teach their daughter. It has been her goal to have the children brought up to be disciplined and well behaved—their son to be courteous and their daughter to be kind and modest.

The merchant's wife is a very busy woman.

GOOD WORKS

Medieval Facts

A wealthy clothier from the city of Bath, William Phillips, founded the Hospital of Saint Catherine and completely restored Saint Catherine's Chapel in Saint Mary's Church. Saint Catherine was the patron saint of spinning—an ideal guardian for a cloth town.

The merchant has always been aware that, in theory, the church looks down on profit making—even though the church makes money in all kinds of ways. He knows Saint Jerome's saying: *Homo mercator vix aut nunquam potest Deo placere* [*The merchant can seldom or ever please God*]. He must please God in other ways. And he is determined to please God, to be sure of his place in heaven after death.

Nobles and a bishop distribute charity to the needy, including a man on crutches (left) and a pilgrim (right).

The Afterlife

He thinks a great deal these days about the afterlife, for which, as the church teaches and he believes, this life on earth is only a brief time of preparation. There is a well-known saying that he repeats grimly to himself: *Salvandorum paucitas, damnandorum multitudo*—[Few are saved; many damned].

The least he can do to help his soul is to go on a pilgrimage. Merchants he knows have been to Canterbury, Rome, Jerusalem, and Spain, to the shrine of Saint James at Santiago de Compostela. He chooses to do penance by traveling to Compostela. His wife will take care of his business affairs.

The accounting books of the Italian merchant Datini record frequent payments of alms, or charitable gifts. Here is one entry:

❖ *March 27, 1395. 1 lira… to give, for the love of God, to a poor woman whose son is in prison and will shortly need to have his leg cut off.* ❖

His charity also emerges in letters like this one to his wife:

❖ *I hope to send you a bale of herrings and about a thousand oranges. You must sell half the oranges and give the other half to whomever you please. And the same with the herrings, or, if you please, give away all the herrings and oranges, the greater part to God in alms, the rest to kinsfolk and friends, rich and poor.* ❖

A close friend praised his charitable practices:

❖ *I think there are more than twenty-five families now alive thanks to you—and God. You give help to more than a hundred a year.* ❖

Pilgrimage to Spain

In April, he dons the pilgrim's robe. He takes the pouch with thread and sewing needle, the coins of gold and silver, the staff, and the plain hat. For all pilgrims, these items symbolize the bindingness of charity and the sharpness of penance. Silver is for grace, gold for glory, the staff for the wood of the cross, the cloak for His humanity, and the hat for the Crown of Thorns. They

A group of pilgrims sets out.

journey "in Christ." He knows the roads well enough, and the inns. The group of pilgrims is from all sections of society, except the poor, who always have to work. He returns feeling that a place in heaven may be his. The long, long journey leaves him tired, but fulfilled.

In the following year, when he is less strong, he pays a priest to go to Rome, the center of the Roman Catholic Church, to stay there for a year, praying for his soul.

Endowments

The merchant also wishes to be remembered more publicly in the town as a religious man. He gives money to various churches in the region and a great deal to his own church. He pays for church repairs and to make the church bigger. It is agreed he and his descendants will be buried there. The charity is sincere, but it is also what most merchants do. Charity is considered not only to be spiritually good for the giver but strengthens claims to the reward of an afterlife in heaven.

HEALTH AND DIET

The merchant's father and mother, and one of his children, died in the first and most terrible outbreak of plague that swept along the trade routes of Europe. The dread of plague fills everyone's mind. Everyone believes that religion and health are the best defenses against it.

An apothecary weighs out the ingredients of a remedy for one of his customers.

Diet

Eating and drinking healthily have always been important considerations in the merchant's family, but it has become more so as he ages. The merchant talks and writes a good deal about his health and food. He eats only two meals a day and usually skips breakfast. Sometimes he enjoys the luxury of a little bread and water or—to keep away the plague—wine. Dinner, the first meal, is at about 10 in the morning, after an hour or two at work. Supper is at sunset.

He has been lucky in many ways. No broken bone has needed setting. No bladder stone has needed removal. He has no cataracts in his eyes. He has had teeth taken out, painfully, when his remedy for toothache didn't work.

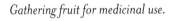

Gathering fruit for medicinal use.

The Doctor

His doctor checks his pulse and his urine regularly. Occasionally, during times when he has caught an infection or become exhausted, he has been prescribed treatments such as *aurum potabile*—a drinkable gold liquid—and pills of powdered stag's horn or emerald. He distrusts these expensive remedies though, believing doctors prescribe them only to rich clients.

His doctor's recommendations for staying healthy include diet and exercise. It is wise to take a little exercise before meals—keep a block of wood and a saw handy. It is wise to wait for two hours after eating before going to bed. Avoid rich foods. Never eat pies.

Avoiding Stress

The doctors say peace and quiet are also essential to health. The merchant should take care not to be upset by barking dogs or noisy neighbors. It is also bad for the health to take matters too much to heart and feel angry, though an occasional burst of fury and shouting is a healthy release.

His health, despite good advice and the care of his wife, is not as good as it was. He is sick from time to time. He needs a stick to walk and eyeglasses to read.

The traveling doctor loses no time checking a patient's urine.

THE END

The merchant has died on his farm while wandering in the vineyard. On his last journey home to his house in the town, he is laid on a bier in a cart hauled by old packhorses. He is accompanied by a priest; six poor men carrying candles walk on each side.

The Wake

The wake is held in the church where his body lies. The funeral bier is draped in black cloth. Twenty or more priests, clerics, choristers, family, and about 60 poor men and women gather around his bier. They all sing from their psalters and chant prayers for the dead merchant's soul.

A great crowd of people is needed. Their prayers are needed to support his soul and speak up to heaven for it, as evidence of the merchant's goodness. All who are there will receive a gift.

All members of the guild are expected at the wake. There are regulations to ensure his wake is observed properly. In his will, he

The merchant lies on his lonely deathbed as God calls him to heaven.

Bequests

John Burghard from Lynn, England, gives instructions for bequests and gifts of money for the upkeep of churches and—as befits a merchant—roads and bridges:

❖ *Towards the fabric of the chapel of St. Nicholas, 10s... [as well as] ...towards the fabric of 6 other local churches. [He leaves] ...20s towards the repair of Setchey causeway and money for repairs also to Stoke bridge.* ❖

A wealthy merchant's funeral is a solemn but grand affair.

important people, and beer for the others. Seventy servers look after them all.

The merchant leaves his house, lands, and property to his widow. He has detailed all the particular objects that will be hers: beds, silver, cloths, tapestries, carts, cattle, and various other items.

He is rich enough to leave money for the repair of the church roof, for the carving of a ship in the nave of the church, and for a priest to sing prayers daily for his soul for 10 years. There are gifts of money for various people he has worked with, including his old farmer friends in the Cotswolds, whose good wool he bought for so long.

He asks that a tomb be built, with a likeness of himself on a carved stone bust above it. He is—was— determined not to be forgotten.

has emphasized there should be no masks or mockery. He asks that only his wife dress in black.

The funeral services are grand and solemn. Vespers, or evensong, is held on the evening before the funeral. Matins are held early the next morning, followed by the mass for the dead. He is then buried in the churchyard to the ringing of the bells of his church and two nearby churches.

The Feast and the Will

At the feast that follows, there is an abundance of food (beef, pork, goose, and fish) and drink. There is wine for "the quality," or

GLOSSARY

Arras ❖ a kind of luxurious tapestry made at Arras, in Artois

Artisan ❖ a craftsman or woman, such as an embroiderer or blacksmith

Banns ❖ the priest "calls the banns" for a prospective couple three times asking in church whether anyone objects to the marriage

Betrothal ❖ being engaged to marry

Bier ❖ a coffin and its stand

Burgess ❖ a wealthy and respectable inhabitant of a town

Chapman ❖ from "cheap," meaning bargain or haggle; a small-scale seller of articles of various sorts, usually a traveler

Crusader ❖ a person (usually a knight) who went off to fight in one of the many "holy wars" against Muslims in the Middle East during the medieval period

Dowry ❖ the money and goods a father gave his daughter when she married

Endowment ❖ a gift of money usually to a religious or educational foundation

Fair ❖ lords were "granted" fairs to allow the sale of goods of all kinds and entertainment in one place

Feudalism ❖ the system of holding land in return for agreed services or work

Fulling ❖ hammering the finished cloth to smooth it, an increasingly mechanized process in late-medieval times

Grammar ❖ rules of a language

Guild ❖ an organization of members of a certain craft with rules for working and for the production and sale of materials

Handfasting ❖ clasping of the hands in betrothal

Herbal ❖ made of herbs

Mass ❖ the main religious service of the church, enacting the ceremonial consumption of bread and wine, "the body and blood of Christ," sung by the priest in Latin

Midden ❖ a rubbish heap

Money ❖ pounds (£), shillings, and pennies, or pence, were the main coins used in Britain in medieval times. A mark was a coin worth 13 shillings, 4 pence.

Mystery play ❖ a biblical story acted out by members of a craft guild

Payment in kind ❖ payment with articles of produce such as eggs

Plighting troth ❖ making a promise to marry

Pounds ❖ *see* money

Primer ❖ a small handwritten manuscript with extracts for children to learn to read from

Sack ❖ a measured quantity of wool

Sarpler ❖ a quantity of wool, about half the amount of a sack

Serf ❖ an unfree person tied or bound to land they hold from another person

Shillings ❖ *see* money

Shop ❖ usually a house with the downstairs used for trading and selling through the window or opening at the front

Staple ❖ an arrangement for buying and selling at particular places, usually towns, making the collection of customs easier and more reliable

Subsidy ❖ a tax in kind; on wool, it would be a certain amount of wool

Wake ❖ the ceremony of keeping watch over a dead person's body prior to burial

Yarn ❖ wool that has been spun into strands

Useful Medieval History Web Sites

www.fordham.edu/halsall/sbook.html

A Web site where you can read many original documents.

http://www.learner.org/interactives/middleages/

A user-friendly Web site on medieval town life, religion, homes, clothing, arts, and entertainment.

http://www.medieval-life.net/famines.htm

This Web site provides information on medieval history, life, family, and literature.

www.mnsu.edu/emuseum/history/middleages/contents.html

Enter this Web site and choose a guide (knight, merchant, nun, or peasant) or topic and learn more about medieval life.

Note to parents and teachers:
Every effort has been made by the publishers to ensure that the Web sites in this book are suitable for children, that they are of the highest educational value, and that they contain no inappropriate or offensive material. However, because of the nature of the Internet, it is impossible to guarantee that the contents of these sites will not be altered. We strongly advise that Internet access be supervised by a responsible adult.

ca. 1000	Europe experiences a great expansion in its population.
1066	William of Normandy invades England and is crowned king in December.
1088	The papacy splits; there are now two popes.
ca. 1090	A weaver's guild is established at Mainz.
1096	The First Crusade begins.
1107	A trade guild is set up in Burford, Oxfordshire. This may be the first guild in England.
1135–1154	Civil war breaks out in England.
1146–1254	The Second through Seventh Crusades occur.
ca. 1150	European rulers grant cities the right to hold markets and fairs.
ca. 1190	The first windmills are built in Europe.
ca. 1200	Money rents replace labor services across Europe. There is a growth in towns, trade, and the economy. There is an increase in the supply of coins and a demand for luxury goods.
1208	King John quarrels with the pope who bans church services in England.
1209	Cambridge University is founded.
1214	Barons demand a charter of liberties from King John.
1265	Marco Polo travels to the Far East.
1275	The first customs duty on the export of wool and leather is levied.
1279	England introduces new silver coins.
1285	Spectacles are made in northern Italy.
1291	Genoese vessels try to sail around Africa.
1294	King Edward takes control of the English wool trade.
1317	Europe experiences heavy rain and ruined harvests; famine spreads across Europe.
1323–1328	The peasants revolt in the Netherlands.
1337	The Hundred Years' War between England and France begins.
1344	The English make their first gold coin.
1346	Calais (an English city at this time) establishes a staple town for English wool trade. All wool must pass through it.
1348–1349	The bubonic plague (Black Death) spreads through Europe.
ca. 1350	The first marine insurance contracts are made.
1357	A long-distance courier service is set up by 17 Florentine companies.
ca. 1360–1400	There is a decline in the export of English wool.
1361	Europe experiences another outbreak of the plague.
1369	Harvests fail across Europe.
1381	The Peasant's Revolt occurs in England.
1437–1438	Many parts of Europe experience the plague and famine.
1438–1440	England experiences heavy rain and ruined harvests.
ca. 1450	Printing with moveable type is invented.
1450	The French defeat the last English army that is sent to Normandy.
1450–1471	The War of the Roses occurs in Britain.
1498	Vasco da Gama lands at Calicut, India.

INDEX

These are the lists of contents for each title in *Medieval Lives*: